Soul Thang

Copyright © 2022 by Lisa R. Dennis.

ISBN:	Softcover	978-1-6698-3418-2
	eBook	978-1-6698-3419-9

All rights reserved. No part of this book may be reproduced or transmitted in any form or by any means, electronic or mechanical, including photocopying, recording, or by any information storage and retrieval system, without permission in writing from the copyright owner.

Amplified Bible (AMP)
Copyright © 2015 by The Lockman Foundation, La Habra, CA 90631. All rights reserved.

Scripture quotations marked KJV are from the Holy Bible, King James Version (Authorized Version). First published in 1611. Quoted from the KJV Classic Reference Bible, Copyright © 1983 by The Zondervan Corporation.

The Message Bible
Scripture taken from The Message. Copyright (c) by Eugene H. Peterson 1993, 1994, 1995, 1996, 2000, 2001, 2002. Used by permission of NavPress Publishing Group.

Scripture quotations marked NIV are taken from the Holy Bible, New International Version®. NIV®. Copyright © 1973, 1978, 1984 by International Bible Society. Used by permission of Zondervan. All rights reserved. [Biblica]

Scripture quotations marked NKJV are taken from the New King James Version. Copyright © 1982 by Thomas Nelson, Inc. Used by permission. All rights reserved. NLT

Any people depicted in stock imagery provided by Getty Images are models, and such images are being used for illustrative purposes only.
Certain stock imagery © Getty Images.

Print information available on the last page.

Rev. date: 06/16/2022

To order additional copies of this book, contact:
Xlibris
844-714-8691
www.Xlibris.com
Orders@Xlibris.com
844000

Soul Thang

Lisa R. Dennis

CONTENTS

Chapter 1   Soul Leaking..1

Some Churchgoers are gathered around the front of the church just before the services starts. Only with itching ears can you wait to hear what they have to say.

Chapter 2   Soul Speaking...6

In church during the Testimony service with the same outside folks on the inside with the same old soul challenge. It's a soul culture.

Chapter 3   Soul Thang 19

After Church back at it again reflecting and talking about it all again. The Reflection

Chapter 4   A Soul Is Reaching Out 26

Friends (very special) talking on the telephone about old times. Billy and Stephanie (Sissy) Stevens grew up together. They fell in love and then grew apart, but the love never faded. Billy has become very successful, but he has an emptiness inside. Deep inside, it's hard for him to love or trust anyone. So, he calls Stephanie his friend who was a beauty queen, wore the latest styles and had a new toy every week. She learned over the years to put up a good front, but secretly, she was trying to find a true relationship with God. She was trying to hide her emptiness until Jesus came into her life and filled all the empty spaces.

Stephanie is on her way into the church when she meets Billy on his way to pick up a Bible from Alvin.

Introduction

soul
/sōl/

A soul is the spiritual or immaterial part of a human being, regarded as immortal. It is the spiritual part of a person believed to give life to the body. Soul is the part of a person that some people believe continues to exist in some form after the body has died. Your **soul** is the part of you that consists of your mind, character, thoughts, and feelings.

Soul or psyche (Ancient Greek: ψυχή psykhḗ, of ψύχειν psýkhein, «to breathe», cf. Latin ‹anima›) comprises the mental abilities of a living being:

thang
/THaNG/

Thang is an altered spelling of *thing*. A thang is a thing that is notable characteristic. Thang is the thing that matters.

Soul Thang is a story about a young lady who has a love for God and a love for her childhood friends to be saved from temptations and devices of the world. Her love for God caused her to have a strong desire to see her friends walking in faith with God.

She knew that it is important today to distinguish the true God from the many false gods of our world. A consideration and review of God's character will help one worship the true God rather than a god of our imagination. It is a thought that we need to consider seeing God as He is so that God can hold the position that He deserves. We need to explore the character of God because it should be the greatest pursuit of our lives. There should be nothing that we need more than to know God in an intimate and personal way. It was the prophet Jeremiah who wrote, "Let not the wise man boast of his wisdom or the strong man boast of his strength, or the rich man boast of his riches, but let him who boasts boast about this: that he understands and knows me, that I am the LORD, who exercises kindness, justice and righteousness on earth, for in these I delight." (Jer. 9:23, 24 King James Version) There is nothing that is more important or more valuable. There is no knowledge that is more significant than this, knowing God is the strength of one's life, knowing God gives one direction and focus. Knowing the unchanging true God in a personal way is life-changing and transforming.

Chapter One

Soul Leaking

What does it mean to have a leak in your soul? Picture this, some Churchgoers are gathered around the front of the Church just before the services starts. Only with itching ears can you wait to hear what they have to say. Just in case you might be wondering, churchgoers are congregants or people who attend worship service but might not be there necessarily to worship God. Some people attend just to see what is going on. On a bright sunny day, three sharply dressed from head-to-toe members of **Humble Sanctuary Fill In Your Church** were engaging in hot and juicy conversation just before church service started and the first Gossiper or spreader of the good rumor and update engages in spilling the tea. They start the conversation with giggles and a hush. **Sister Melba Gasper** struck up the conversation "Child, did you go to the service the other night? Well, child let me tell you. Sis. Kay showed off!" **Sister Sangria Sipper replied, "**You don't say." Very eagerly instigating and anticipating more good rumors and updates. **Sister Melba** says, "Well, she come walking in like she own **Humble Sanctuary Fill In Your Church**, you know to sit in her favorite seat. She struttin her stuff like she some peacock and know good and well she just want to sit up in Bro George's face!" Now, Sister **Gabby Piper** has something to add to the dish. She inserts "Child, Sis. Dorothy wears her dress so short that Bro. Pastor must come off the pulpit to preach!" **Sister Sangria**

Sipper, yelped out, "God ain't calling for all of that foolishness and that kind of behavior." **Sister Gabby** adjoins further and says, "Did you see Sis. Smith shouting after she was with Bro. Jim last night?". Now the question that I have is, how did she know where Sister Smith was last night? **Sangria Sipper** replies, "She got some nerve." **Melba** yelps, "Yea, Sis. Joan was kicking too as soon as the music stopped, she suddenly stopped too!" **Sangria Sipper** attaches to the discussion, "Child, you know Sis. Joan don't have no Holy Ghost. She just actin a fool." This lady starts mimicking and acting just like Sister Joan going through the same motions and all. **Alberta Riper** intensifies the conversation with "Child, did you see Sis. May's hair?" **Sister Sangria Sipper** says, "You know she can do better than that." They look at each other and hysterically laugh! They hear the music and singing starting in church. The choir is singing, "Thank You Jesus, thank you Jesus, thank You Jesus, I wanna thank You!" Sister Sangria Sipper says, we'd better go inside before prayer start. You know we don't want nobody to say we are gossiping." **Sister Alberta Riper** says, "Yea, child, I know what you mean. The Saints will label you in a minute." And they walk inside the church join in singing with the choir, "You woke me up. You woke me up. You woke me up! I wanna thank You!" Thank You Jesus. Thank You Jesus. I wanna thank You."

What do you do when you have a leak in your soul? What do you do when you feel empty inside? Do you retreat into a hole, waiting for someone to pull you out? Do you deteriorate into a TV junkie/lazy person/Facebook addict? Do you lash out at anyone and everyone who dares to enter your space, including the dog? Do you keep pressing forward, struggling with what feels like running through waist-deep water? Some people find comfort, rest, and peace in the house of worship. Busy-ness, parenting pressures, financial stress, illness, difficult people, or any of the other normal pressures of life can poke holes in your internal vessel and leave you with an empty soul. And if your internal level of stash is already low, a larger-than-normal leak in your soul can quickly drain any remaining strength you have. Your creativity dissolves, you don't handle even minor stresses well, and you struggle to see anything positive in the world even in the House of Worship.

You can learn the warning signs that indicate you are running on empty. When you let small things really upset you, sometimes to the point of tears. It is a warning sign that usually happens just before you get there. The warning sign comes to show us that we need to get intentional about filling up. This fill up can happen in a Worship Service.

When your stomach is empty you find something to eat. Sometimes it's a quick snack – the healthier the better. Sometimes it's a gourmet meal. Your body does best when you regularly eat a variety of good quality food. But what you *don't* do when you're hungry is sit down and wait for someone else to feed you. Unless you're in four-point restraints and in solitary confinement, you feed yourself. It may take effort. You may not be able to immediately get your favorite meal. There are an infinite variety of foods that may satisfy your empty belly. But *you* still must feed yourself.

It works the same way with an empty soul. It may take effort. You may not be able to immediately get your favorite soul nourishment. There are an infinite variety of activities and thoughts that may satisfy your empty soul. But here's the key: *You must learn how to make sure you feed your own soul.*

That doesn't mean you create soul food out of nowhere, or that all soul food is equally nourishing. But it does mean that *you* are the one who must proactively choose to look for and intake whatever nourishment your soul needs.

Where to Find Soul Food

Your soul needs many kinds of nourishment. It's important to be aware of what nourishes you; it's as unique as the kinds of physical food you like and don't like. Here are a few categories to think about.

- **Quietness vs. Inspiration.** Most of us in today's world are overstimulated. We face constant input from television, smart phones, and social media. That kind of data overload drains your internal bucket. Going non-digital for an hour, an afternoon, a weekend, may revolutionize your sense of being refreshed.

- **Organic vs. Synthetic.** Our lives are often filled with everything man-made, buildings, cities, media, noise, pollution. Much of it is very good, some not so good. But when your soul needs to be filled up, there's something about nature that meets a need nothing else can. The sound of rain, a bird song, the feel of sand under your feet – it reminds you of the Creator who made all that, and *you are* too.

- **Inspirational vs. Performing.** Most media capitalizes on the sensational, the superficial, or the scandalous. The entertainment value of it may keep you "mentally unresponsive," but it won't fill your soul. On the other hand, there are certain books, movies, music, or even TV programs that truly lift, fill, and enlarge your soul in a big way. You can tell the difference by the effect your inner heart experiences.

- **Natural vs. Everlasting.** Things we can see, feel, and touch are important. God created the Garden of Eden as a very physical place. But you and I were created for more than this earth. We were created for forever. Time spent reading Scripture, in prayer, in worship alone or with other believers, or just being in silence in the presence of the Lord – these nourish the part of your soul that only God can fill.

Don't think it strange when your body needs food, or that some foods lead to better health than others. So, ask yourself these similar questions about how you nourish your soul.

1. **How do you know your soul is empty?** What are your unique emotional signals? How do you behave differently when your soul is depleted? What tells you you're running on empty?
2. **What soul food is most nourishing to you?** When do you feel most alive, most refreshed, most creative? What people, activities, or places fill you up?

Continuing to run on empty will never turn out well. Notice the signals that indicate you have an empty soul and learn to feed yourself with the nourishment you need. Notice what fills you up and find ways to do more of that.

What signals tell you that your soul is running on empty? Can you name one or two things that provide you with soul nourishment?

Chapter Two

Soul Speaking

The Sister Ladies in Chapter One were not the only ones experiencing soul leaking but the good news here is that they all were in the right place at the right time to hear soul speaking from the soul reaching source which is The Word of God. These Sisters were in Church during the Testimony service. The same outside folks on the inside with the same soul challenge. You do remember testimony service, don't you? I remember being in Church service one Sunday and a lady wanted to testify but she said, "I don't know the poem." "I want to say something, but I do not know the poem." What is the poem…. You know, first giving honor to God, who is the Savior of my soul and head of my life. Giving honor to the Pastor of this Church, pulpit associates, officers, members, and friends. That was referred to as the poem. The opening introduction used just before you proceed to tell your experience of what the Lord has done for you. **Sharing or telling your testimony** is telling about your relationship with God and what He is and or has done in your life. One of the greatest witnessing tools we have available to us is the testimony of a changed life. We can look at many examples in the Bible of people who came to Christ, were saved, and walked away changed. That same thing is happening today. You have the ability to share your story of a changed life. When sharing your Christian testimony through spoken word you want to remember that while this is a blessing to those who are saved, it can be used by God to reach the unsaved. Always speak with the thought in mind that unsaved people will be listening to your testimony. Before you begin to testify, pray. Take time to talk with the Lord about speaking your testimony. Each opportunity is a witnessing tool that God can use to touch a life. Allow Him to guide your words. Tell about your miracle, blessing or what brought you to the realization of your need of a Savior. You don't need to give a laundry list of your sins, but you should tell how you were brought to conviction and share the solution. When you are done with your testimony everyone should know that it was God through Jesus and that He is the answer to their problem of sin. Your salvation is not what you were able to accomplish on your own, but it was purchased by Jesus on the cross (Titus 3:5-7) "Not on us abundantly by works of righteousness which we have done, but according to His mercy He saved us, by the washing of regeneration, and renewing of the Holy Ghost; Which He shed on us abundantly through Jesus Christ our Savior; that being justified by His grace, we should be made heirs according to the hope of eternal life." Focus your testimony on pointing people to Jesus.

Be careful about using words that unsaved audience members won't know. The longer you are saved, and the more time you spend in Church, the harder it is to remember that people outside the Church don't understand all our vocabulary. Also remember that other religious groups use the same words we do in Christian Churches but have a different meaning to their vocabulary. The more you can give your testimony using common words, the clearer your communication will be. Stay focused and try to give the important elements of your testimony clearly and in a few words. If you have time or space, you can give more information that will help illustrate your points. But don't waste precious time telling stories that won't help people know about how the Lord drew you to Himself or brought you out of your situation.

It is very important to always be honest. Share your testimony in an honest way. There is no reason to sensationalize or lie about the events in your life. Just because other people may have been saved out of a horrible background and you haven't, doesn't mean you are any less saved. There will be people in the audience who can relate to your real story, even if it sounds boring compared to someone else's testimony. When you are honest God can use your words to reach others. Make sure that you share your current situations. What is God doing in your life today? It is great to hear what He did last year (or 30 years ago) in saving you, but your audience will want to know that God is still at work in your life today.

stay within the allotted or reasonable time. If you are told you have 3 minutes to give your testimony, then you need to stay within that time limit. This shows respect to your hearers and those speaking after you. If the listeners know you only have 3 minutes and you speak for 7 then it can be seen as boastful on your part. Make sure you honor God the one who saved you when you share your testimony with others. It might even be helpful writing your Christian testimony out. It can help to keep you focused and also it is a wonderful way to share the miracle of a changed life with the hearer.

Always be ready to tell your testimony. You may think that because it's your story, you don't have to do anything to be ready to tell it. After all, you were there when it happened, and you're living it now.

But you can get nervous, become side-tracked or forget things when you're sharing your testimony, which can be confusing or distracting for those listening. This is why a little preparation and practice can be so valuable.

The Testimony Service is beginning, and **Sister Sangria Sipper** testifies, "I thank the Lord that I am truly saved and filled with the Spirit of the Holy Ghost not just any ghost, but the Holy Ghost. Because people fail to realize that God sees all. All that we do (looks over at Mrs. Smith). Yawls pray for me that I will forever be real for the Lord." And the Church said, "Amen!"

Sister Gabby Piper "Saints, I tell you God is so good just before service the sisters and I were talkin about the goodness of the Lord and how it you can't say nothin good about somebody, don't say nothin at all. Cause truly God has some beautiful people. And I just love you all."

Sister Alberta Riper pops up and testifies, "I thank the Lord for saving me. Most of all for filling me with the Holy Ghost. I am just so grateful that I keep to myself and mind my own business. Those of you who know the words and worth of prayer, pray much for me." Here goes **Sister Melba Gasper** with a word or two, "Be kindly affectioned, one to another, with brotherly love in honor preferring one another. I truly thank the Lord for God's word. Because when one sister is being affectionate to one another's husbands, they just doing what the Word says. And it ain't none of my business. Ya'll pray for me."

After Testimony The Ministry Of Music

As the testimony portion of the service is ending the ministry of music is going forth with a selection from the **Church Choir: I Need Your Spirit.** The choir is in place in the choir stand. All sopranos, altos, tenors, basses, baritones, monotones, mesto, contralto's those in between and trying to find their notes, were all present and prepared to sing for worship. The musician's organist, pianist, keyboardist, drummer, bongo and conga, tambourine, bass guitar, lead guitar, saxophonist, trumpeter, flutist were all on one according playing in the key of C and the choir began to sing the words to the song. "I need Your Spirit! To speak to my spirit. Words of life, comfort, and peace. I need Your Holy Spirit! To speak to my spirit. Word joy that bring sweet relief. Holy Spirit! Holy Spirit! Holy Spirit, I need You this hour."

There is no fog machine to give the allusion that the presence of the Living God is there. It is evident by the lifting of the hands and the countenance and the expressions of joy the Lord is in this place.

Music Ministry Defined. A Church ministry is an action or service that is done in response to God's call on a person's life. The music ministry **uses music in some way to serve God.** Music is very powerful in its effect on the human emotions. Music Sets the Mood.

The Purpose of the music, worship, and creative arts ministry is to help provide an atmosphere, which is suitable and comfortable to worship. The members of this ministry must apply their godly discernment in choosing, playing, and singing the right songs, dramatizing the right plays, and using liturgical dance movements at the right time. They must see to it that all the choices of music, songs (lyrics), dance movements, and drama pieces meet the right priority of worship: first, to glorify God; second, for God to speak to us; and third, for us to edify each other.

The motivation for establishing the music, worship, and creative arts ministry is to:

- Help create a worship environment in all the events of the church
- Help create a worship atmosphere during all group rehearsals
- Help create a mindset for all the members to become worshipers
- Help promote professionalism in the arts of music, dance, and drama in the church
- Help promote proper training of the musicians and singers.

Someone has to take the lead, guide or facilitate the service they are called in some churches the Worship Leader, Presider, Minister in Charge (the MC) or as Humble Sanctuary Fill In Your Church the one is called **The Church Announcer In Charge.** The Church Announcer is the one who will lead and guide the service by announcing what and or who will be next on the program. The program can be written or unwritten. The Announcer proclaims," We will now have our offering!" offering is a form of worship and in our worship, we want to be found giving. Though the Announcer is in charger of guiding the service at most churches and houses of worship it is the deacon or one who handles the money who will take over from here.

The ministry of a deacon. Nowadays, as in the early Church, the role of a **deacon** may encompass a variety of services differing from denomination to denomination. In general, **deacons** function as servants, ministering to the body in practical ways. They may assist as ushers, tend to benevolence, or count tithes and offerings. No matter how they serve, Scripture makes it clear that ministering as a deacon is a rewarding and honorable calling in the Church.

The biblical role of Deacons is to take care of the physical and logistical needs of the Church so that the elders can concentrate on their primary calling.

Deacons must be well respected and have integrity. They must not be heavy drinkers or dishonest with money. They must be committed to the mystery of the faith now revealed and must live with a clear conscience. Before they are appointed as deacons, let them be closely examined. If they pass the test, then let them serve as Deacons.

Deacon Everly Downright shouts and dances up to the pulpit microphone and exclaims, "In order for the church to run, it's gotta crawl." The Church replies, "Let it crawl, Deacon, let it craw!" And after the church crawls, it's gotta walk." The church replies, "Let it walk, Deacon let it walk!" After the church walks, it's gotta run." The Church replies, "Let it run, Deacon, yes, let it run!" In order for the Church to run, we need some money." **The Humble Sanctuary Fill In Your Church** replied, "Let it crawl, let it crawl! Deacon Everly Downright standing in confidence and faith replies, "Saints, do your level best to make the church run." The Church is all in tunned with what the deacon is saying until he requires them to give their money. **The Church replies, "Let it Crawl!"**

Deacon Everly Downright grabs the microphone and leads the church in a giving song We got to have the money! **The Deacons** Stands Up and begin to proclaim, "We got to have the money!" the Humble Sanctuary Fill In Your **Church joins in and** Everybody Standing getting their money out and opening their purses and pockets) Singing, we got to have the money…..... we got to have the money!

When the ministry of giving is done in a liberal way that people are giving as unto God (walking away after offering with a shout), they will give without restraint.

The ministry of giving is the practice of systematic and proportionate giving of time, abilities, and material possessions based on the conviction that these are a trust from God to be used in His service for the benefit of His Kingdom. It is a divine-human partnership, with God the senior partner. What My **Giving** does. It meets the needs of people, and it makes people whose needs are met to bring glory to the name of God.

Now back to the rest of the service. The Church Announcer announces, "We will now have our welcome." **Deacon Roger Dodger** says, "Good Morning Sis. Evangelist, Pulpit Associates, Officers, Members and visiting friends. We would like to have all of our visitors stand at this time. (Stand up, I mean you) We the members of the Humble Sanctuary Fill In Your Church would like to welcome you to our simply divine, fine church where nobody has the audacity to doubt that somebody insinuates that anybody prevaricates, we welcome you."

The importance of the welcome in Church. One of the key things that people value more than anything else from their vicar and from their church, is warmth and welcome. It is the church's welcome that will **most encourage people to return to church, and to develop their faith and trust in God**. Not surprisingly, a lack of feeling welcome is the experience most likely to drive them away. Some people never come back to church simply because they did not feel welcomed. The word "welcome" means "gladly and courteously received; agreeable or gratifying.". By definition, then, a welcoming church graciously receives its people in a kindly way. To welcome someone is an act of charity, and therefore it is a beneficence that has a legitimate place in the life of the Church.

Now, returning to our regular scheduled service as the choir starts to Sing "The Great I Am" He's Alpha and Omega the beginning and the end. The first and the last, the forgiver of your past. Surrounded by angels who praise Him both night and day. There is no nobody bigger that can put Him out. The Great I Am. Yes, He is the Great I Am. He's!"

Just as the Spirit continues to ascend. It appears that someone has to draw attention to themselves. What is an attention seeker? An attention seeker is someone who acts solely in a way that is geared towards garnering the attention of other people. Persistently Bragging. Attention seekers are very good at showing off their achievements, even if what they're telling you about isn't really an achievement at all. Always fishing for Compliments. Attention seekers are constantly looking for reaffirmation of who they are, or who they perceive themselves to be. Professional Victims....Constant Complainers.

Resuming to our service, you remember **Deacon Roger Dodger**, he starts singing terribly (I don't know why the Lord keeps blessing me) and the **Announcer:** (*Interrupts*) I don't know why either, but we thank the Lord for our choir and the mask singer I mean the worst singer. Now we will have what we all have our Church Announcements. How important are the church announcements? **Church announcement** s are **important** to have in every church as they inform about the upcoming events and activities in the church, issued for the public interest. Even though every **Church** has them, not many can do it properly. They have to be compelling and interesting enough for people to listen to them.

The one who gives the church announcements at Humble Sanctuary Fill In Your Church is the Church Clerk. (The Church Clerk's Job Is to give the morning announcements. She is really proper and wears glasses.)

Church Clerk Gloria Gathers properly says, "Good Morning saints, ain'ts and friends. Greetings and God bless you. It is my pleasure to read for you the church announcements. As some of you know, there will be a board meeting Monday of this week with the following boards – Deacon's Board, Men's Day Board, Women's Day Board, Usher's Board, Mothers' Board, checkered board, ironing board and everybody else's board. On Saturday afternoon there will be a picnic, fashion show, dance recital, tea and luncheon and choir rehearsal.

Next Saturday Bro. Marvin Glover and Sis. Janice Dixon will be united together in holy matrimony. [All of this time they've been doing the married thing, I thought they were married.] Will they please stand? [Forgive them God for they know now what they do.] You may be seated.

On Friday there will be water and fire baptism. [You know some of you need to get baptized all over again. God is not pleased with your living!

Prayer meeting on Tuesday night. The theme is "It's me, it's me O lord, standing in the Need of Prayer" She adds her two cents, [I don't need to be at this service.] Anyway, Wednesday night is regular Bible Study. There's Sunday School, New Members Class, Sunday Morning, and evening services.

Remember, your soul is a terrible thing to waste.... Hey, Glory! (Shouts her way to her seat) and the Church says, "Amen!"

The Announcer continues with the service program "Now, we have come to the part that we have been waiting for! Everybody stand and receive our Pastor. The Preacher of the hour.... the soul Reacher.... The Bible Teacher.... Reach in each Each!!!!! "(Shouts his way to his seat) As the Preacher takes to the pulpit.

Reverend Icha Nod The Preacher approaches the pulpit, and all of the congregation stands up to honor him, he exhorts the Church, "Good Morning! I said Good Morning to you! You can be seated if you can! I just want to share a little bit of the Word with you this morning!

I would like to declare the Word of The Lord to you this morning by choosing as my subject that There are Three Classes among the Lost according to the book of Acts 17:30-32) "And the times of this ignorance God winked at; but now commanded all men everywhere to repent.: Because he hath appointed a day, in which he will judge the world in righteousness by that man whom he hath ordained; whereof he hath given assurance unto all men, in that he hath raised him from the dead." And those three classes are…they are "Neglectors, Rejectors and Despisers".

The Word of God makes it plain that all mankind out of Christ as lost. But there are different classes among this vast multitude. I want us to consider at least three of these classes. The purpose for doing so is that we might cause some that belong to these classes to think upon their ways and turn to God before it is too late. First, there are the neglectors Hebrews 2:3 "How shall we escape, if we neglect so great salvation, which at the first began to be spoken by the Lord and was confirmed unto us by them that heard him." All that one has to do to be eternally lost is just do nothing about being saved. John 3:18 "He that believeth on him is not condemned: but he that believeth not is condemned already, because he hath not believed in the name of the only begotten Son of God." This is true because: Man by nature is a sinner and is lost (Romans 5:12) "Wherefore, as by one man sin entered into the world, and death passed upon all men, for all have sinned." As a sinner, he is unfit for heaven. "And he saith unto me, Seal not the sayings of the prophecy of this book: for the time is at hand. "He that is unjust, let him be unjust still: and he which is filthy, let him be filthy still: and he that is righteous, let him be righteous still: and he that is holy, let him be holy still. And behold, I come quickly; and my reward is with me, to give every man according as his work shall be. I am Alpha and Omega, the beginning, and the end, the first and the last. Blessed are they that do his commandments, that they may have right to the tree of life and may enter in through the gates into the city. For without are dogs, and sorcerers, and whoremongers, and murderers, and idolaters, and whosoever loveth and maketh a lie." (Revelations 22:10-15) and cannot enter in (Revelations 21:27) And there shall in no wise enter into it any thing that defileth, neither whatsoever worketh abomination, or maketh a lie: but they which are written in the Lamb's book of life.

As a sinner, he is sure of hell according to (John 8:21, 24) "Then said Jesus again unto them, I go my way, and ye shall seek me, and shall die in your sins: whither I go, ye cannot come." Vs 24 I said therefore unto you, that ye shall die in your sins: for if ye believe not that I am he, ye shall die in your sins."

Second, there are the rejecters. A rejecter is one who things he is good enough and does not require anything from Christ.

This is true of many Jews in the day of Paul (Romans 10:1-3) "Brethren, my heart's desire and prayer to God for Israel is, that they might be saved. For I bear them record that they have a zeal of God, but not according to knowledge. For they being ignorant of God's righteousness, and going about to establish their own righteousness, have not submitted themselves unto the righteousness of God."

This man is in Matthew 22:9-14 but we don't have time to look "Go ye therefore into the highways, and as many as ye shall find, bid to the marriage. So those servants went out into the highways, and gathered all as many as they found, both bad and good: and the wedding was furnished with guests. And when the king came in to see the guests, he saw there a man which had not on a wedding garment: And he saith unto him, Friend, how camest thou in hither not having a wedding garment? And he was speechless.

Then said the king to the servants, bind him hand and foot, and take him away, and cast him into outer darkness, there shall be weeping and gnashing of teeth. For many are called, but few are chosen." The man without the wedding garment has deliberately refused the garment. He is the type that would be saved by their own doing (Titus 3:5) "Not by works of righteousness which we have done, but according to his mercy he saved us, by the washing of regeneration, and renewing of the Holy Ghost;"

Third, there are the despisers (Acts 17:32-33) "And when they heard of the resurrection of the dead, some mocked: and others said, we will hear thee again of this matter. So, Paul departed from among them." These are those that "mock" at the gospel. (Acts 17:32)

Those that ridicule the miracles such as the resurrection from the dead.

Those that consider themselves to be wiser that God and His Word "For the wisdom of this world is foolishness with God. For it is written, He taketh the wise in their own craftiness. And again, The Lord knoweth the thoughts of the wise, that they are vain."(I Corinthians 3:19-20), (I Corinthians 1:18-21) "For the preaching of the cross is to them that perish foolishness; but unto us which are saved it is the power of God. For it is written, I will destroy the wisdom of the wise, and will bring to nothing the understanding of the prudent. Where is the wise? where is the scribe? where is the disputer of this world? hath not God made foolish the wisdom of this world? For after that in the wisdom of God the world by wisdom knew not God, it pleased God by the foolishness of preaching to save them that believe."

Sinners that neglect, reject and despise can be saved only if they would turn to Christ before it is too late (John 1:6-10) "If we say that we have fellowship with him, and walk in darkness, we lie, and do not the truth: 7 But if we walk in the light, as he is in the light, we have fellowship one with another, and the blood of Jesus Christ his Son cleanseth us from all sin. 8 If we say that we have no sin, we deceive ourselves, and the truth is not in us. [9] If we confess our sins, he is faithful and just to forgive us our sins, and to cleanse us from all unrighteousness. [10] If we say that we have not sinned, we make him a liar, and his word is not in us."

You can count them one…two…three!!! The Neglectors, Rejectors and Despiser. The doors of the church are open. Is there one? Is there one who has thought on his wicked ways and humbled himself and turned to righteousness? Is there one this morning?…….. Two? ………. Three?…….or four?

During the altar call appeal. People respond to the Inspiring Preached Word of God full of hope and faith. Reverend Icha Nod Preacher says, "Choir give us a selection." And the choir sings melodiously song: **I Am What I Am by the grace of God. By the grace of God, I am what I am. I am saved. I am healed. I'm forgiven and Holy Ghost filled.**

The Choir Sings and then Church is over as everyone precessions out except for the Gossipers. They remain)

Do you remember being in an inspirational setting and when it was time to leave, can you remember what remained? What where your thoughts about what inspired you at that time?

Chapter Three

Soul Thang

After Church the ladies are back at it again reflecting and talking about it all again. I do not think that this kind of behavior is only reflected in women. I do believe that men have gatherings and this manner of speaking sessions as well. Since this storyline is geared to the attention of these ladies, we will focus our attention on what happens next.

Melba Gasper starts off by saying, "Child that sure was a good service!" (Hands waving in the air) **Gabby Piper** joins in as usual by saying, "Yes, and deed! Yes, and deed it was! (Still in the spirit) **Sangria Sipper** chimes in, "Pastor sure did pa-reach! **Alberta Riper says,** "He sure did!"

Melba Gasper says, "I don't know what he preached! But he sure did preach!"

Alberta Riper (pointing across the way in the opposite directions) "Is that Sister May in the wrong car again?"

All Ladies: "Child!!!!!! Child!!! Child!!! Child!!"

Gabby Piper "Neglector!"

Alberta Riper "Rejector!"

Sangria Sipper "Despiser!"

Melba Gasper "Neglector! Rejector! Despiser!"

These Ladies go on about their way and continue to fellowship in the Humble Sanctuary Fill In Your Church. Every opportunity to fellowship in the traditional service, they found themselves there. It is something about the traditional church service that drew them.

What Can You Expect In A Traditional Church Service?

In a Traditional Worship service, you will typically have a **choir** and a **choir leader** or director. The choir will typically sing in unison with the congregation using hymnals. The hymnal, by the way, is that book which is usually sitting right next to you or directly in front of you during the service.

The typical length of time for a Church service is anywhere from one to two hours. Many churches have multiple worship services, including Saturday evening, Sunday morning and Sunday evening services.

Most worship services begin with a time of praise and singing worship songs. Some Churches open with one or two songs, while others participate in an hour of worship. Twenty to thirty minutes is typical for most churches. During this time, a choir arrangement or a particular song from a solo artist or guest singer may be featured. The purpose of praise and worship is to exalt God by focusing on him. Worshipers express love, gratitude, and thankfulness to God for all He has done. When we worship the Lord, we remove our eyes from our own problems. As we recognize the greatness of God, we are lifted up and encouraged in the process.

After the time of praise there is usually an official greeting or welcome. The greeting is a time when worshipers are invited to meet and greet one another. Some Churches have an extended time of greeting when members walk around and chat with one another. More typically, this is a brief time for greeting the people directly around you. Often new visitors are welcomed during the greeting.

Most worship services include a time when worshipers can give an offering. The receiving of gifts, tithes, and offerings is another practice that can differ widely from Church to Church. Some churches pass around an "offering plate" or "offering basket," while others ask you to bring your offering forward to the altar as an act of worship. Still, others make no mention of the offering, allowing members to give their gifts and contributions privately and discreetly. Written information is usually provided to explain where offering boxes are located.

Some traditional Churches observe Communion every Sunday, while others only hold Communion at determined times throughout the year. Communion, or the Lord›s Table, is most often practiced just before, just after, or during the message. Some denominations will have Communion during praise and worship. Churches that don't follow a structured liturgy will often vary the time for Communion.

A portion of the worship service is dedicated to the pronouncement of the Word of God. Some Churches call this the sermon, the preaching, the teaching, or the homily. Some ministers follow very structured outlines without variance, while others feel more comfortable speaking from a free-flowing outline. The purpose of the message is to give instruction in the Word of God with the goal of making it applicable to worshipers in their daily lives. The time frame for the message can vary depending on the church and the speaker, from 15 to 20 minutes on the short side to one hour on the long side.

Not all Christian Churches observe a formal altar call, but it is common enough to make mention of the practice. This is a time when the speaker gives the members of the congregation an opportunity to respond to the message.

For example, if the message focused on being a godly example to your children, the speaker may ask parents to make a commitment to strive toward certain goals. A message about salvation may be followed by an opportunity for people to publicly declare their decision to follow Christ. Sometimes the response can be expressed with a raised hand or a discreet look toward the speaker. Other times the speaker will ask worshipers to come forward to the altar. Often a private, silent prayer is also encouraged.

Although a response to a message is not always necessary, it can often help to solidify a commitment to change. Many Christian Churches like to offer an opportunity for people to receive prayer for their specific needs. Prayer time is typically at the end of a service, or even after the service has concluded.

Before I finish, most Church services end with a closing song or prayer.

In a traditional Church service, you are most likely to see or be greeted by Deacons (dressed wearing suits and big crosses) not be ne mistaken by the preacher. The Preacher (male or female) usually stands out above the others in the congregation of the church members. Church Members (some of the women sitting in the rows of the pew often wearing hats and men on the opposite side dressed in their Sunday's best suit attire.)

Children usually are accompanied by their parents, grandparents, godparents, relatives, or neighbors. Church Ushers are on their post.

A Church usher is a **person who helps ensure a smoothly running church service and who ministers to people in a variety of practical ways**. The specific responsibilities of an usher vary with the Church, but their duties usually include greeting people as they arrive for the service, assisting people with special needs, and receiving the offering. **Ushers** in the tabernacle and temple were called doorkeepers. The psalmist understood the importance of **ushers** when he said, "Better is one day in your courts than a thousand elsewhere; I would rather be a doorkeeper in the house of my God than dwell in the tents of the wicked." Psalm 84:10 (King James Version)

The Church Nurse is usually present to provide **support to the Ushers** during Church service, Only If Called Upon. Perform duties as assigned by the Pastor. Assist at funerals. When assisting the emotionally aroused person, the Church Nurse should first defer to the Usher. Note: Remember that crowd control is most important when attending to the needs of a person who integrate faith and healing to promote wellness within the community they serve.

A Church Clerk, the Choir, the Devotions – led by the Deacons, Processional – Ministers and the Choir are all part of the traditional church worship service experience. – "Holy, Holy, Holy Lord God Almighty!"

In the traditional Church worship service experience, there is an Order of Service. The **order** of **Service** is always under the supervision of the Holy Spirit and thus, subject to change at any time. There is a Call to Worship. A call to worship is an **invitation for the congregation to turn their attention toward God**. It's typically not intended to be a lengthy intellectual discourse but a summons. Then immediately following the call to worship is the Hymn of Praise. The hymn of praise In Christianity, hymns are directed to the one true God, of course. God's people have sung hymns in honor of the Almighty since the time of Moses and before (Exodus 15:1) "Then sang Moses and the children of Israel this song unto the Lord, and spake, saying, I will sing unto the Lord, for He hath triumphed gloriously: the horse and his rider hath He thrown into the sea."

Announcements in the traditional worship service are anointed and appointed to inform the congregants about upcoming events. Church announcements are important to have in every church as they **inform about the upcoming events and activities in the church**, issued for the public interest. Even though every church has them, not many can do it properly. They should be compelling and interesting enough for people to listen to them – usually declared by the Church Clerk.

Throughout the traditional worship experience the Ministry of Music is interwoven from the beginning to the end of the service. In my estimation, the most important musical part of the service. It is the voice of the whole church lifted to God in praise and adoration, or in supplication. Music comes to man's help when speech seems insufficient. So, music should be considered as an intensifier and beautifier of thoughts and emotions.

Just as all aspects of ministry is important during the traditional worship experience the Ministry of Giving usually administrated by the church Deacons. The ministry of giving has many goals: **spreading the gospel, sustaining the church, providing and care for distressed individuals.**

All aspects of the traditional worship experience serves to address and meet the Cares and Concerns of the congregants. The sermon is meant to provide spiritual food for your spirit, soul, and mind.

The Sermon invites **us to reflect and** to connect with God's Word and to invite you to a closer relationship with Him. The Invitation is an extension of the preaching time and should give the audience an opportunity to experience what has been presented in the message. At the end of the traditional worship experience, sometimes the congregation finishes the final hymn as this **recessional** takes place, but sometimes the attendees are led out **during** the last verses. This may be a formal process. The Recessional and Benediction As nouns the difference between recessional and benediction is that **recessional is music played** during a church recession while benediction is blessing (divine or supernatural aid, or reward). For many churches, the **benediction** is the final act of worship. The preacher or pastor stands before the gathering, with hand extended over the congregation, and closes the **service**. It means a **blessing**, a greeting, an expression of kindness and love. **Benediction** is also a beautiful part of the **church service** in which the congregation receives a prayer of blessing pronounced by the preacher over the attendees.

It is no wonder that the Ladies and members of the Humble Sanctuary Fill In Your Church can't wait for the opportunity to fellowship and praise the Lord together. What about, you? What is your reason for fellowship and praise to God?

Chapter Four

A Soul Is Reaching Out

All souls belong to God, Ezekiel 18:4 "Behold, all souls are Mine; the soul of the father as well as the soul of the son is Mine; the soul who sins shall die." The souls of the dwellers in Heaven belong to God. Each and every order of spiritual existences, from the lowest who waits before the throne, to the tallest archangel in the hierarchy of Heaven — belongs to God; for by Him, says the apostle, "were all things created, which are in Heaven and in earth; whether they be thrones, or dominions, or principalities, or powers." **God** owns you! Your soul is not your own; you **belong** to another. **God** owns you by right of creation. Because he created you, he owns you--just as any artist owns that which he creates. But some don't know it yet. **All souls belong** to you. But some don't know it yet.

Meanwhile back to our soul thang story, though we began the story with a traditional church worship story, the real beginning of the story started over thirty (30) years ago with friends. – Friends (very special) friends talking on the telephone about old times. Billy and Stephanie (Sissy) Stevens grew up together. They fell in love and then grew apart, but the love never faded. Billy has become very successful, but he has an emptiness inside. Deep inside, it's hard for him to love or trust anyone. So, he calls Stephanie his friend who from what he would remember was a beauty queen, wore the latest styles and had a new toy every week.

She learned over the years to put up a good front, but secretly, she was trying to find a true relationship with God. She was trying to hide her emptiness until Jesus came into her life and filled all the empty spaces.

True friends are hard to come by these days. Growing up, I was told that everyone is not your friend. I was told that you can choose friends, but you cannot choose your family, so choose your friends wisely.

A friend is someone who doesn't pressure you to do things you don't want to do. Nothing is better than a night in with some good food and gossip. If you're feeling pressure from your friends to go out every night and put important things, like homework and studying, to go out, they may not truly be friends.

A friend is **someone that you share close affection with.** You share some common beliefs and values with friends. Friends can be in person or online, your next-door neighbor friend or a friend 1,000 miles away. Often, a friend is someone you trust or enjoy being around. Some friends are casual; you may talk sometimes. You're closer to other friends.

A friend is **someone who doesn't dump you and who helps you when you get hurt.** Someone who says they are sorry when they do something to hurt your feelings. ...

A friend is **a person who will suggest and render the best for us regardless of the immediate consequences.**

Stephanie is thinking about her childhood and her friend Billy. She is looking at pictures and singing "Billy Boy." The telephone rings and the answering machine picks up. She hears Billy's voice and picks up. Their conversation begins....

Stephanie: Hello

Billy: Hello, how are you?

Stephanie: Wait, this can't be William Nathaniel Brown Jr? Would you believe that I was just thinking about you today?

Billy: Really, Isn't that something.

Stephanie: Where and how have you been?

Billy: Fine, just fine. I saw your friend Sheila and asked about you and she gave me your number. I told her that I really needed to get in touch with you and how I hoped to see you soon.

Stephanie: What have you been up to? It's been so long since I've heard from you.

Billy: Oh, nothing. Working hard, trying to stay alive. That's all, I guess.

Stephanie: Where are you now? It's so good to hear from you.

Billy: I'm back in town for a while. Looking for an out-of-town job. God only knows I need to get away… (*sigh*)

Stephanie: Did you ever finish school?

Billy: No, but I have a chance to go back.

Stephanie: That will be nice. I always said you'd make a fine businessman.

Billy: I don't know about all of that… (changing the subject). Well, how is your family?

Stephanie: Everybody is doing fine.

Billy: And how are you, Sissy?

Stephanie: I'm doing fine. In fact, I am blessed.

Billy: Blessed? What's this blessed stuff? You're not one of those fanatic Jesus people, are you?

Stephanie: I don't know what your idea of a fanatic Jesus person is, but I can only tell you the difference He's made in my life.

Billy: Well, I can see that you're very serious about your relationship with the Lord.

Stephanie: More than that, Christianity is a lifestyle for me, and I am more excited than I've ever been before. I have peace, joy, and an abundance of love. Can you understand that?

Billy: Sissy, before I believe anything and anybody else, I believe you. You were always a special person, not like anyone I've ever met. You always know what to say. I've been a lot of places and seen a lot of people, but I can't compare any of them to you. I remember when we were kids. We would laugh and play. Then, we grew up. We had to grow up, didn't we?

Stephanie: we did have a lot of fun, didn't we? Remember when we were little kids? Life was so simple.

Chapter Five

Little Souls Looking And Reaching Back

It appears that this young man is reaching back. His soul is looking back to wonder how he got over. I remember when we were children and playing was the number one thing on our mind. We would think about what we would play, who we would play and who we would play with. We would play outside and inside. We had things to play with and even if we didn't have anything to play with, we would use our imagination to play. Those were days of innocence and love. Life was simple back then. Boys grew up to be men and little girls grew up to be women.

There is one thing that I remember from that traditional church. The Humble Sanctuary Fill In Your Church church, that just like God is interested in your soul, so is the devil interested in your soul and your future. We were taught that the devil is out to steal, kill and to destroy your soul but God is present to give you life more abundantly. It is specially noted that we realize and understand that the same devil, enemy of our soul that is out to steal, kill and destroy the adults has no respecter of persons, places or things and is out to steal, kill and destroy babies, children, teens, and young adults. Children need the same information and ministry that adults need in an age-appropriate way.

EVANGELIZING CHILDREN AND YOUTH OR Doing The Work Of An Evangelist Among Teenagers

"Nevertheless, I will remember my covenant with thee in the days of thy youth, and I will unto thee an everlasting covenant". (Ezekiel 16:60)

The word **"teenager"** has become more than just an age group; it is a new way of living and thinking. Teenagers have emerged as a separate culture within their culture all around the world. Their values, their language, their problems, are unique.

The enemy seems to have focused his attack on young people with one objective in mind; to spiritually neutralize one entire generation. If the devil can create one generation without God, he can have all the generations to follow.

The enemy is not the only one who has plans for today's teenagers. "In the last days", God says, "I will pour out my spirit on all flesh (people). Your sons and daughters will prophesy, your young men will see visions…."

(Joel 2:28; Acts 2:17)

The enemy is fighting with formidable weapons of music, media, videos, games, doomsday thinking, brightly packaged sin, and family erosion.

God has entrusted us with the challenge of crossing generations with the gospel. How shall we respond?

It will require a willingness to change where needed and a commitment to creativity. If we try to reach this exploding generation the same old way, we will be talking to the same old people.

They are a generation hungry for a leader, liberator, a savior, and hero. We need only to present Christ in their language, and multitudes will follow Him.

Because teenagers are high energy people, short program segments are most effective. Remember, keep things moving. An effective program is held together by a theme from beginning to end.

The recipient (lost teen) of the package (Jesus and all His blessings) moves from the familiar, to the friendly, and progressively to the message. First, you want them to feel at home. Secondly, you make them ready to receive. Thirdly, make them think about Christ.

If a young person without Christ wanders into the meeting, they must hear the gospel presented clearly, attractively, and persuasively. He or she may never pass this way again.

The central facts of the Gospel – man's sin, Christ death and resurrection, man's response – are clear and unchanging. The communication question becomes – how do I state the Gospel in terms that a non-Christian teenager will best understand?

Ultimately, Christianity is a person, not a system, nor belief, nor a religion. Marriage can be considered a system or an institution, but ultimately it boils down to; "what do you think of this person"? Christianity is that kind of personal choice.

Teenagers are attracted to Jesus. They may resist or ignore the Bible, Christian ideals, Christian morality; but there is something compelling about the person of Jesus Christ. Make Him the issue in your preaching to teenagers. Lean heavily on the Gospels in preaching to them. There, they will learn in flesh-and-blood what Christ expects and how He treats people.

Young unbelievers object to hypocrites in the Church, mistakes made in Christ's name, and inconsistencies. But most objections are put to rest with the simple clarification – "it is Christ I am asking you to follow, not Christians". What is it that you object to? Paul said there was no issue, "except Jesus Christ, and Him crucified". (I Corinthians 2:2)

Everywhere in the world, young people equated God with a religious system, Buddhist, Catholic, Moslem, etc. The details are different, but the basic idea is the same; perform for God.

The Gospel, on the other hand, emphasizes knowing God – as father, master, and friend. We are inviting teenagers to begin a relationship, not to join a religion.

Unfortunately, when we say "God", most teenagers hear "religion". Our communication challenge is first to establish that our message is a person… and secondly, that it is possible to have a relationship with that person.

In fact, the Gospel can be clearly explained to teenagers in relational terms. They can understand that emphasis can be explained this way:

- You are God's unique creation, designed to enjoy a personal relationship with Him. (Psalm 139:14) "I will praise thee, for I am fearfully and wonderfully made. Marvelous are thy works and that my soul knoweth right well."

- Sin keeps you from experiencing that relationship between you and God. "For all have sinned and come short of the glory of God; being justified freely by His grace through the redemption that is in Christ Jesus," (Romans 3:23-24); "Behold, the Lord's hand is not shortened that it cannot save, neither His ear heavy, that it cannot hear. But your iniquities have separated between you and your God, and your sins have hidden his face from you, that he will not hear." (Isaiah 59:1-2)

- Jesus Christ died to make possible a relationship between you and God. "But God commended His love toward us, in that, while we were yet sinners, Christ died for us." (Romans 5:8); "For there is one God, and one mediator between God and men, the man Christ Jesus." (I Timothy 2:5)

- The relationship begins when you respond to what Christ has done for you. "But as many as received Him, to them gave the power to become the sons of God, even to them that believe in His name." (John 1:12)

We are proclaiming to a lost teenager the relationship he/she was built for, the relationship he/she is looking for, and the one relationship he/she can depend on.

The Gospel is "Good News". But it makes no sense without the bad news. A cure for a disease is meaningless if I do not acknowledge or care about that disease. So, sin is a central issue in the Christian message. Without it, the "cure" of Christ's death does not seem very important.

With moral boundaries disappearing in many parts of the world, many teenagers have little sense of being "out of bounds". They have very little feeling of having violated any laws, especially since there is great confusion over whether the laws apply anymore.

So, when talking and ministering to the youth, you are faced with the challenge of communicating the seriousness of sin to a morally casual generation. That is done by emphasizing three (3) facts concerning this moral cancer called "sin".

First, we must emphasize the damage sin does. Teenagers may not acknowledge the disease of sin. But they cannot deny its' results. They can see what selfishness, greed, and insensitivity are doing to their world. Each Evangelist asks young people, "where do you think all this comes from"? He/she then answers, "from a moral disease called sin – a disease that infects us all". The damage done by sin is more than societal…it is personal. A young person should consider the guilt he/she feels, the people they hurt, the scars and regrets he/she cannot shake. In us, and around us, we can see the ugly marks of this disease we all carry.

Second, a teenager can understand sin by recognizing the reason it kills. The earth was built to revolve in orbit around the sun. From the sun, it receives warmth and light, and life. But, if the earth suddenly wandered into an orbit of its' own, away from the sun, all warmth and light, and life would cease.

You and I were built to live in orbit around God. He is the source of the love, the light, and the life we must have. But we have lived in our own orbit, away from God…" Each of us has turned to his own way" (Isaiah 53:6). We are out of orbit, drifting without purpose or care. If we die away from the Son, all life will cease.

Thirdly, our sin message should emphasize the "Missingness" of God. The God we were built for is on the other of the wall. The "wall" is sin. We keep trying to fill the hole in our hearts with some pleasure, achievement, or relationship – but that voice keeps whispering, "something is missing". Our message to teenagers is that "that something" is a "someone".

Teenagers need a sense of specialness in order to feel excepted. Around the world, teenagers question their worth. Without worth, there is little motivation to live significantly, to keep yourself clean, and to respect others. Our Gospel must emphasize that every teenager is a unique, hand-made, one-of-a-kind creations of God (Psalm 139:13-18). He/she is not just a face in the crowd, or a collection of atoms.

If a teenager thinks he/she is trash, he/she will throw his/her life away (drugs, alcohol, no goals, immorality, etc.). If he/she thinks he/she is expensive, he/she will keep himself/herself special. We base the specialness on two (2) Gospel facts.

- God made you.
- God paid for you…you are very expensive. "For you are bought with a price: therefore, glorify God in your body, and in your spirit, which are God's." (I Corinthians 6:20)

Teenagers Need A Cause To Live For

Teenagers today know that someone must make a difference in their family, their school, their society. That is why the "Follow Me" of

Jesus Christ is so compelling. He offers the love and power that are so desperately needed to keep us from destroying each other. Christ is the cause our restless hearts were built to serve.

A young person will simply live for himself/herself – to survive and feel good…unless he/she is challenged by the Jesus alternative. The kingdom He proposes to build is an exciting cause in a self-centered world. We should emphasize to teenagers that Christ offers more than a "born again" experience…He offers a "transforming" way of life. A person…relationship…a moral disease…a sense of specialness…a cause to live for – those are Gospel emphases that can capture a lost teenager's heart. It all flows from a cross and an empty tomb – that is the Gospel. When those profound events intercept a teenager at the point of his/her need, he/she will never be the same again.

Each Teen Should Develop And Experience:

A Life of Prayer: Young people especially teens need to have this area in the life fulfilled. As Youth Evangelist, we are to encourage teens to pray one for another and for the needs they may have.

A Life of Praise and Worship: Teens may enjoy music and desire to offer them God's best. We encourage them to participate in praise and worship to the Lord. We also desire them to have a life of praise to the Lord. Christian music that gives glory to the Lord is encouraged.

A Life of the Word of God: God's Word is essential to teens. It will give them power and the ability to stand on all of God's promises. We encourage Bible study and confession of God's Word.

A Life of Evangelism: We encourage the youth meetings to be an outreach to their friends, peers, and neighborhood. We also believe that teens go and win souls to the Lord. (Teens beget other teens to the kingdom).

A Life of Fellowship: Fellowship is important to teens. They need to know that they can come together and enjoy each other's company. Activities are planned and entire group participation is encouraged.

Life experiences in all of these arenas in the life of a youth will help to make them well rounded and rooted in their faith.

There is nothing wrong with reaching back and remembering when you were young as long as the reach back is the making of a comeback that will bring glory to God.

There have been many days that I find myself reminiscing. Recalling the days of yesterday. Pondering of years ago. Especially pleasant memories. If you are swapping old stories with friends and remembering all the silly things you used to do, then you're **reminiscing. Reminiscing is** all about happy recollections and thinking back to stories from the past.

It's okay to reminisce. I used to think because I would **reminisce** that meant I was still stuck in the past which to a point is true but it's more harm than good to repress your thoughts. This **nostalgia** is good for us in more ways than one, research shows. **Reminiscing** helps us feel better about the present and more hopeful about our future.

Reminiscing isn't just a nice thing to do, it's been proven that it can make us feel physically warmer about ourselves. When we do it; we also feel more hopeful about our futures and emotionally closer to those around us." This was certainly true for these friends, who loved sharing their memories together.

Whether you reminisce over a phone conversation with a good friend, pour over an old photo album, or have a keepsake created from your clothes with special memories, one thing's for sure – we all need to make time for reminiscing.

I remember that we use to play and sing songs like:
Little Stephanie Ann, sitting in the sand
Weeping and a crying over Billy man
Oh, won't you rise sister Stephanie
Wipe your dirty eyes
Roll your rollie cheeks
Shake it to the East
Shake it to the West
Shake it to the one that you love the best

We would sing and jump rope to songs like:
Not last night, but the night before
Sissy met Billy at the candy store
He brought her ice cream, he brought her cake
He brought her home with a bellyache
Momma, Momma I feel sick
Call the doctor quick, quick, quick
Doctor, doctor will I die
Just close your eyes and count to five
1 – 2 – 3 – 4 – 5 I'm alive

We would sing and play hand games to:
Sissy and Billy sittin' in the tree
K-I-S-S-I-N-G
First comes love
Then comes marriage
Then comes Billy with the baby carriage
How many babies will they have?

Many times, while the girls were playing separately by themselves the boys would come and interrupt. (Little Billy and his friends come in while they're playing and picks on them). It was just like those boys to come and disrupt our games because secretly they wanted to be included.

What good memories do you have from your childhood? Can you remember any and are you in contact with any of your childhood friends.? Do you pray for them? Do you know if they are keeping you and your family in their thoughts and prayers?

Chapter Six

Souls Teens Making Plans

Back to our story "Soul Thang", there are Soul Teens making plans for the weekend during the days before everyone had their own phone there was the house landline telephone that everyone used. Stephanie would spend countless hours, days and years talking on the telephone (Landline) with her friends.

Her friend Vanessa: (*dials Stephanie's phone number. Stephanie's mother Mrs. Sharon Stevens answers*) Hello Mrs. Stevens. Is Stephanie home?

Mrs. Stevens: Stephanie is here somewhere, Vanessa. She is supposed to be doing her work, but she says she can't do a lot of work because she was born premature. Hold on. I'll get her for you. Stephanie, Vanessa's on the phone. I hope you're talking about church and school and not those boys.

Vanessa: See, why can't my mom be that nice to me. Here, I have to sneak to use the phone before I do my work. I'm moving in with Stephanie. They don't know it yet.

Stephanie: Hey Ness. What's up?

Vanessa: Nothing compared to what's up with you and Billy.

Stephanie: Girl what are you talking about? Don't even try it.

Vanessa: Trying it is not wat I'm talking about. It's what you've done girlfriend.

Stephanie: Vanessa what are you talking about? You've been doing your science experiment too long and your brain is damaged.

Vanessa: I heard that you and Billy had a C.P.R. lesson by the library today. I'm talking mouth to mouth lip action.

Stephanie: It wasn't even like that. Who told you anyway?

Vanessa: I cannot reveal my informative, lowdown, inside story, hearsay informant because they would kill me. So that's why I wanted to find out the real truth from you – my best friend.

Stephanie: Yea right. It was just an innocent kiss for good luck in the basketball game tonight. That's all.

Vanessa: Did he hold his arms around you?

Stephanie: Yea.

Vanessa: Did you kiss long?

Stephanie: Not really long.

Vanessa: What were you wearing?

Stephanie: My jeans and a school shirt and Billy's basketball jacket.

Vanessa: What was he wearing?

Stephanie: Jeans, a sweatshirt and his other basketball jacket.

Vanessa: Oh, this is so romantic.

Stephanie: Girl, you are crazy. You have completely lost your mind.

Vanessa: Are you going to the game tonight?

Mrs. Stevens: Stephanie are you still on the phone?

Stephanie: Yes, mom.

Mrs. Stevens: Alright. Remember you need to finish your work.

Stephanie: Alright Mom. I'm back Ness.

Vanessa: So, what about the game?

Stephanie: That's just it. Billy wants me to meet him after the game, but I'm supposed to come straight home after the game.

Vanessa: Well, let him walk you home.

Stephanie: He is walking me home

Vanessa: You mean…hold it…I have an idea. Maybe you can say you're staying the night with me.

Stephanie: That just might work. She'll let me stay over your house and that way I can spend more time with Billy, and she would never find out.

Mrs. Stevens: (*overhearing – walking in and says*) She'll never find out what?

Stephanie: Bye Vanessa. I'll talk to you later.

Mrs. Stevens: Much later.

Vanessa: Okay, Good luck.

Mrs. Stevens is **a model parent**. Like in most households where parents are present and disciplining and setting boundaries for their children are the norm. They set firm household rules and behavioral standards. Responsible parents usually Communicate with their children and instilling values. They model positive behavior and responsibility for their children. They foster love and affection with their children. Those model parents praise them for things they do well and correct and instruct them in the direction that they should move forward all in the name of family and love.

Mrs. Stevens is **sticking close** to her daughter Stephanie because she wants her to know that she loves her daughter and that she has her best interest at heart. (*They walk out of the room together hand and hand*). **Mrs. Stevens says** What do you mean "She'll never find out?"

Stephanie: Not that you won't find out, or that you don't find out or that you shouldn't find out…

Mrs. Stevens: Haven't I told you time and time again, whatever you do I will know about it one way or the other? Either way, I find out.

Stephanie: Well Mom, it's like this. Remember when you were young like my age, and you were very beautiful? In fact, you're more beautiful no that you were then. Do you want me to cook dinner? How about moping the floor? That's it. I'll clean the whole house and wash and iron all the clothes. You're really the best Mom anybody could have. You're very, very understanding.

Chapter Seven

Soul Dance

This "soul thang" is a thing as we continue, two friends, Sheila and Stephanie go to a dance party. Sheila talks Stephanie into going. She doesn't really want to go. Her heart is not in it because she knows she will feel out of place. Sheila persuades her into going. This part of the "Soul Thang" starts with a conversation of persuasion and then the party begins. **Persuasion is** the ability to influence other people's thoughts and opinions using convincing arguments and facts. Persuasion is also the process by which a person's attitudes or behavior are, without duress, influenced by communications from other people. One's attitudes and behavior are also affected by other factors (for example, verbal threats, physical coercion, one's physiological states). Not all communication is intended to be persuasive; other purposes include informing or entertaining.

Sheila tells Stephanie, "There's a dance tonight and every fine thing in Humble will be there. I'm in love under new management honey! (As she imagines herself getting hooked up with a love connection tonight at the party.) **Stephanie** encouraging her friend, "Well, I hope you have fun flaunting your flesh around."

Sheila says, "What you mean "You hope I have fun?" You're going with me I can't let you miss this. No matter how boring you are. You've got to have one exciting memorable event to tell your grandchildren."

Stephanie: I'm not going. You know I don't dance.

Sheila: What you mean "You don't dance?" This is me you're talking to. You taught me how to (and she *does a dance move*) dance.

Stephanie: Well, I don't dance anymore.

Sheila: Come on. You don't have to dance. Just go. Who knows, my baby just might find his way home.

Stephanie: Girl, you are too much. I probably should go just to keep you out of trouble.

Sheila: Come on. You know you want to go. (*She pulls her along*)

Just to make the record straight, there is nothing wrong with a party and for the most part dancing is not a sin. Everyone knows that the party doesn't stop when the music stops, and it doesn't stop when you leave the venue. A good party can last a lifetime and so can a bad one. Good music and good preaching are good to the soul.

Dance allows you to let yourself go and express how you feel through movement. **Dance** is a transformation of time, people, space, and feelings. **Dance** is about stepping on stage and leaving it all on the floor. Dance is prayer - when you don't have the words to say simply dance and your heart will express the word your heart wants to say.

Dance is meditation. According to Marieke Van Vogt, writer of the article "The Mediation of Dance. Dance allows you to be in the moment. In ballet class your mind can not …

Dance provides an escape. Momentarily you can escape from the harsh realities of whatever it is through recreational, interpretive, or expressive dance. The best spiritual connection is the connection we have with others. When our spirits align, and we experience movement together it provides the bliss we seek in the spirit of fellowship. The magical feeling of connecting to others in a higher dimension through the art of dance is what heightens the spiritual experience. It's metaphysical. Through dance you develop an "unconditional bond" with other dancers, with the audience—and when you touch the heart of others through the art of dance an emotional bond occurs.

One of the major components of dance is healthy living. A healthy body enhances a healthy mind. Health and spirituality go hand and hand. In the article "Spirituality and Health" it is mentioned that the mind, body, and soul are connected, and the health of the body affects the health of the mind.

Dance and movement help to provide emotional support and there are even dance therapy programs. So don't just sit there! Dance and discover your own inner spiritual awakening!

The (*Party starts and is jumping. Sheila is ready to party. When they walk in, standing at the door is Billy.*) **Sheila:** (*not so happy to see him*) What are you doing here? (*She goes inside*) Party…Party!

Stephanie: Hi Billy. I didn't know that you would be here.

Billy: Yea. I know the guy that's DJ'ing. He is one of my boys. We go wat back. I helped him bring his equipment over.

Stephanie: So, are you staying?

Billy: For a little while I guess. Do you want to dance?

Stephanie: No, I'm not into dancing these days.

Billy: why would you come to a dance if you're not going to dance?

Stephanie: Don't ask.

Billy: Okay, you want to sit and talk?

Stephanie: I'd like that.

(*The party is almost over*)

Sheila: Why are you spending a lot of your time and all of your time over here with him? He's just one fish. Look at all those other fish in the sea. (She points to the other boys in the room) There's a shark, there's a bass and there's a whale. Watch out for him. And you're sitting here with a tilapia! Girl, you better dance at least once. The party is about over.

Stephanie: I don't think so.

Sheila: You can't say I didn't try. Hey, hey you fine thing. Let's dance!

Billy: She's right about one thing. You should dance just once.

Stephanie: I don't know.

Billy: Come on. There's nothing wrong with this song.

(*They dance to the fast song. It's over and goes into a slow song. They are still dancing. Stephanie feels bad not because she danced, but because she feels out of place.) She stepped out on to the dance floor and wowed them with her dance moves and dance style.*

Sheila: Girl, I saw you. Looked like the old Stephanie I used to know.

Stephanie: Sheila, I feel really bad about tonight and I don't know why.

Sheila: Girl, you didn't do anything wrong. You were just having fun enjoying yourself.

Stephanie: How come I don't feel good?

Sheila: Because you're a square. You're a regular Rubik's cube. That's what you are.

Stephanie: Oh, you don't understand. Not you. Not Billy. Nobody understands. She walks out) Stephanie is feeling very emotional. She feels the pull of her lower nature and there is a struggle and question within her if she is making the right decisions. She looks inward and says to God, "Lord let Your will be done. Let Your will and Your Kingdom come in me. Not my will but Your will be done. Not my way but Your way be done. If it is even possible in my life and in my situation, let Your will be done."

How many times have we been in a situation, that we've questioned if we were doing God's, will and wanted God's will to be done?

Chapter Eight

Soul Reminisce On Repeat

There is something happening and is in motion that is continuing to reach My Friend. This is critical the moment a seed was sown to get Billy to soften his heart and open up to a new and better way thinking and living. **Stephanie** saying to her friend, "That night was the turning point of my life Billy. I knew then that I would never be the same.

Billy: Well, I know that God is proud of you like I am. Maybe more, I guess. Sissy, you have found something that I'd like to find. I think after we hang up, I think I might need to call on the Lord, because I sure could use His help. **Stephanie:** I'm sure He'd be glad to hear from you. And Billy, He's got all the help you need. God loves you very much and so do I. I'd like to see you tomorrow it it's possible.

Billy: I'll call again around 6:00 before I come over. I'm glad I called.

Stephanie: Don't forget to pray and I'll talk to you tomorrow. I promise.

They both hang up from this telephone conversation, but Stephanie turns her thoughts toward God, and starts another conversation; "I can't forget, I won't forget. Lord, when I was down and out, You were there to bring me out. The time I couldn't get relief, You gave me so much peace. I needed healing for my soul, that's when Your Word made me whole and Lord for all You've brought me through, that's why I'm praising You! I can't forget. My mind was so confused. I had been hurt and so misused. I was searching for the truth, and I realized it was You. That is when I began to pray, and You gave me a brighter day. Lord for all You've brought me through, that's why I'm praising You! Lord, I can't forget, I won't forget, and I don't want anything or anybody that will get in the way of that for me."

Stephanie still in prayer, "God, Billy is ready to receive your Son Jesus tonight. He just doesn't know it yet. Take the fear away from him. Lord, if You saved me…. You can Save Billy and Anybody! Maybe he's ready tonight, Lord. He said that he might need to call on you. (*She says this prayer for Billy*) Father, in the name of Jesus, I come before you in prayer and in faith believing. It is written in your Word that Jesus came to save the lost. You wish all men to be saved and to know your divine truth. Therefore, Father, I bring Billy before you this day. Satan, I bind you in the Name of Jesus and loose you from the activities in Billy's life! Father, I ask the Lord of the harvest to thrust the perfect laborer into his path. A laborer to share your Gospel in a special way so that he will listen and understand it. As your laborer ministers to him, I believe that he will come to his senses and come out of this snare of the devil that's held him captive and make Jesus the Lord of his life. Your Word says that you will deliver those for whom we intercede, who are not innocent through the cleanness of our hands. We're standing on your Word and from this moment on, Father I shall praise you and thank You for Billy's salvation. With my faith, I see Billy saved, filled with your spirit, with a full and clear knowledge of your Word. Amen – so be it!

Soul Reminisce On Repeat Again

intercede
[ˌin(t)ərˈsēd]

The act between parties with a view to reconciling differences.

Interceding in prayer, it primarily denotes a **"meeting with,"** **a conversation or petition rendered on the behalf of others**. "Intercessory prayer," then, is seeking the presence and audience of God in another's stead. When we pray for the needs of others that is called "intercession" or we are said to be "interceding" for them.

I Timothy 2:1 "I exhort therefore, that, first of all, supplications, prayers, intercessions, and giving of thanks, be made for all men."

Sister Wanda is praying for the protection and deliverance for the city. Stephanie comes in for guidance and comfort and tells her of her conversation with Billy. **Wanda:** (*praying*) Father, in the Name of Jesus, I've received your power – your ability and might because the Holy Spirit has come upon me and I am your witness in Humble and to the ends of the earth I confidently and boldly draw near to the throne of grace to find help in the time of need, because we in the city need it. Father, thank you for sending forth your commandments to the earth. Your Word runs swiftly throughout Humble. Your Word continues to grow and spread. Father, I seek and request the peace and welfare of Humble where you have caused us to live. I will not let false prophets who are in the midst deceive us. I come against the violence and strife in the city in the Name of Jesus. Holy Spirit, I ask you to visit our city and open the eyes of the people, that they may turn from darkness to light, from power of satan to God, so that they may thus receive forgiveness and be released from their sins. In Jesus name, Amen.

(*Wanda gets up from praying and puts on a praise song. Stephanie, a little upset knocks on the door and Wanda lets her in.*) Stephanie is waiting for

Wanda to let her in. **Wanda** hurrying to the door," I'm coming. Here I come. (*She opens the door*). Hi Stephanie (she greets her with a *hug)* Hi Sister Wanda. How are you today? Just fine thank the Lord.

Stephanie showing up with a lot on her mind but trying not to show her true feelings **says to Sister Wanda** "What a nice day we're having." **Wanda says,** "Sure is. Isn't God good? Sister Stephanie, what brings you to this side of town?"

Stephanie: Oh, Sister Wanda, I talked to my friend Billy last night. You remember him? We've talked and prayed about him enough.

Wanda: Yes, I remember Billy. (*Very concerned*) Is he alright? (*Looking at Stephanie thinking maybe she might be in the family way*) Are you alright?

Stephanie: No, Sister Wanda. It's not like that. And I don't know if I'm alright. I don't think Billy's alright either.

Wanda: Tell Sister Wanda what's on your mind.

Stephanie: How can I reach him? I've just got to reach him. He's hurting inside.

Wanda: I see.

Stephanie: And not just Billy. I look at the many others who started out fighting on the front line tearing down strongholds. Now they're weakened from the battle because Satan came in to kill their lives. How can we reach them?

Wanda: (*Reaches out to hug Stephanie*) We won't let them die. We'll pour the oil of the Holy Spirit upon them. We'll bind up their hurts and cover them with blanket of God's love. We'll minister to them. (*She continues to pray a prayer of intercession) Thank You Lord for healing in this city, thank You Lord for saving by Your grace and thank You Lord for moving by Your power. Thank You Lord for healing in this place. This place* *is holy. This place is holy. This place is holy and filled with Your majesty. This place is sanctified, justified, and set aside for You. This place is holy and filled with Your Majesty.*

A prayer of intercession happens **when one party or person prays exclusively to the Lord God for another party or person concerning some particular state or action.** It's an exclusive prayer to God on the behalf of someone or a nation. Therefore, it goes well beyond just praying to the Lord God on behalf of another.

An intercessor bases his or her requests not on their own merits or on the merits of the one they are interceding for, but on God's compassion. Intercessory prayer is not only a privilege but a command. "Continue steadfastly in prayer" (Colossians 4:2) is an "imperative." "Persistence in prayer is not an option for the Christian" but "an order from the Lord Himself."

The primary principle of intercession is simply to **tell God what** He **tells us to tell Him** as **the means of releasing His power.** He tells us what to pray in His Word. We can pray the promises of God.

Intercession

There are a lot of lost and wounded Souls in the world and even in the Church. Yes, people are hurt, wounded, and serving. There are *people walking through lost, blind, wounded by the cares of this life and sin. They get to the point where someone needs to intercede on their behalf and minister to them. (Ex: fallen preacher with a big cross picking up prostitute, a church Mother shouting one minute and drinking the next.)*

There are people who talk and preach about such people with no remorse or conviction. Some people say that that is what they get for being disobedient. Everyone that is lost, wounded, and hurt are not in that position because of themselves or because of their sin. Some people are bound because of the sins or disobedience of others. This is the reason that we need more intercessions. Those who will stand in the gap for someone other than themselves. I find that we don't talk about or gossip about those that we love, and we pray for on a regular basis.

Are there any people who you find yourself talking about negatively on a regular basis? Can you take a challenge and make a commitment to pray for them for at least 21 days? Make an intercessory prayer list, commit in faith to pray, and watch God do miracles.

Chapter Nine

Soul Witness

Once you commit to seeing God's work done on earth as it is heaven, then you have a strong desire to see good overcome evil and light dispel darkness._This is "Soul Thang" must be taken out to the streets. Witnessing and evangelism happens when there is an answer to the call to evangelize. The street evangelist will pass out tracks. Some want to hear. Others won't. There will be people walking on the street, playing basketball, etc. Billy is drawn in by the gospel rap or the urban revival message and gives his life to the Lord.

The purpose of the Urban **Revival** message is to focus on bringing the **gospel message** to the inner city **with** messages that are relevant to today's culture, **through** spoken word, **gospel, rap,** drama, dance (the **performing arts**) and **preaching.**

The message of the gospel is the same Old and New Testament is the same; turn to God and turn away from anything that opposes Him: the message is straight to the point and simple for all people to understand. This is what the "Soul Thang" message is,

This ain't no game it's a Soul Thang. Don't say you love the Lord if it's not true. Because, darling He cannot stand no lie. God loves you baby, don't live life like you're crazy. The way you do the things you do. God's love for you will never end. If you need a friend, just put your trust in Him. This ain't no game! What it is, it's a soul thang. In the time of trouble. He'll be there on the double. You just call His Name; no need be ashamed. You need to know that His plan for you is true. He made the world; He can deliver you. God's love for you will never end. If you need a friend, put your trust in Him. This ain't no game. It's a soul thang, yeah. Confess with your mouth, what is right and believe in your heart have eternal life. Get you soul right.

Alvin is a street evangelist and happens to have a gift of spoken word and music ability. He uses Christian rap. Christian **rap** is **rap** music that is inspired by the life of Jesus Christ and His teachings from **the Gospel.** Christian Hip Hop is a way of poetically **preaching** the truth of God's word, solely to uplift and evangelize in today's generation. **Can Rap be Christian?** Why am I making such a big deal about rap? Because I love the Gospel. And I know that people like Stephanie Stevens, Billy Brown, Sheila Davis, Vanessa Clark, D, L, Shack, Lady Shady, and Gabby Piper love the Gospel as well. Music is not really the most important issue here; God's truth is most important. So, I am very concerned with how God's truth is presented, delivered, proclaimed, and disseminated. If the *way* that the Gospel is presented contradicts the very message, I am concerned about the integrity of the Gospel. So where does this leave us? Based upon all this analysis, the unavoidable conclusion is that rap music, because of what it inherently communicates, is incompatible with the Christian Gospel. It expresses sentiments that contradict the very message that we love. Alvin is a gifted man of God who has given his life over to the full-time expression of grace through Christian rap.

Alvin: If you were to die today, Billy, do you know for sure that you would go to be with your Father in heaven?

Billy: No, I can't say that

Alvin: The Bible, the Word of God, says that if you would believe in your heart that Jesus died for your sins and that God raised Jesus from the dead and confess with your mouth that Jesus is Lord, you shall be saved. Do you believe that Jesus is Lord?

Billy: Yes, I do.

Alvin: Repeat this prayer after me.

Billy: Okay

Alvin: Father God

Billy: Father God

Alvin: I thank you for loving me

Billy: I thank you for loving me

Alvin: So much that you gave your son

Billy: So much that you gave your son

Alvin: Jesus to die for me

Billy: Jesus to die for me

Alvin: Jesus, Christ, Son of God

Billy: Jesus, Christ, Son of God

Alvin: Come into my heart

Billy: Come into my heart

Alvin: Forgive me of my sins

Billy: Forgive me of my sins

Alvin: Cleanse me from all unrighteousness

Billy: Cleanse me from all unrighteousness

Alvin: And be my Lord and Savior

Billy: And be my Lord and Savior

Alvin: Jesus

Billy: Jesus

Alvin: I declare that you are the Son of God

Billy: I declare that you are the Son of God

Alvin: That you died and rose again

Billy: That you died and rose again

Alvin: And that you are Lord and Savior

Billy: And that you are Lord and Savior

Alvin: of my life

Billy: of my life

Alvin: Amen

Billy: Amen

Alvin: Praise God Billy. You are a new man. Old things are passed away and all things are become new. Now you are in Christ Jesus!

Billy: Thank you Alvin.

Alvin: Now that you're saved, you need to get into a good church and find somebody strong in the Lord.

Billy: I know just the person and she will be so helpful.

Alvin: Well, praise God. If you need a Bible, come to the church today and I'll give you one.

Soul winning is the greatest occupation that any man can be engaged in. There is no greater, no higher calling than winning souls. Soul winning brings the greatest measure of joy which man can obtain from doing things. The joy of winning souls to Christ is of a character that is deep, satisfying, and lasting. This will benefit them more than anything else that can be done for them. Soul winning will bring the greatest reward. This is a work for time and eternity.

After a person is saved and has obtained eternal life, his labors for the Lord will bring reward. Eternal life is a gift we receive when we are saved. Rewards are payments we receive for working for the Lord.

The fighting has been left to a few. It is not the brave, prepared recruits, who are needed, but the trained soldier who is of value to God. The Lord taught us the value of training by His example; in spending much time upon preparation of those who would carry out His work.

Many will be startled when all the workers in His vineyard are gathered before Him in the day of reckoning. The busy mother, the workman in the shop, the farmer, the barber, the merchant, the teacher, the cook, the maid; may receive a greater reward for service, than the pulpit orator, the evangelist, or the missionary.

Soul Winning is the angel coveted work of bringing man to God. The human soul is priceless, and he who engages in this work of rescuing men from sin and hell and winning them to God is performing the most exalted task ever committed to mortal man.

Soul Winning is the Christian's supreme privilege. Neither Gabriel, nor Michael, nor any other angel of heaven is permitted to engage in this glorious task; for the joy of which they would be glad to leave the portals of glory; but it is the privilege of the Christian.

Soul Winning is rescue work, which is emergency work. Joshua, the high priest was called by God, "a brand plucked out of the fire" (Zechariah 3:2). The soul winner is exalted in Jude 23a, to save souls by, "pulling them out of the fire".

Make a list of those souls that you have been praying for and try to reach out and connect with them either by phone, text, letter, card, or in person.

Chapter Ten

Soul Friends Reach

Souls are reached when prayer and faith work together. This is what true victory looks like? not that our prayers are always answered the way we want them to — but that **God is at work even in the difficult parts of our lives**. "The Lord uses our life stories for good, even when it's uncomfortable." We are to love God, our Creator, with all our heart, mind, and soul and we are to love our neighbor as ourselves. That is God's definition of victory for all of us. It does not get any simpler than that.

It is absolutely impossible to live this life in our own strength. Life is precious, but it can also be remarkably difficult at times. Faith is what **helps to get us through**, brightening the pathway in times of darkness, helping to give us strength in times of weakness. Without faith, it becomes impossible to see and obey God.

Hebrews 11:1-3 "The fundamental fact of existence is that this trust in God, this faith, is the firm foundation under everything that makes life worth living. It's our handle on what we can't see. The act of faith is what distinguished our ancestors, set them above the crowd. By faith, we see the world called into existence by God's word, what we see created by what we don't see." (The Message Bible)

Hebrews 11:6 "It's impossible to please God apart from faith. And why? Because anyone who wants to approach God must believe both that he exists *and* that he cares enough to respond to those who seek him." (The Message Bible)

To live by one's faith is to **see God's hand and his holiness** in all calamities and shaking:

Walking by **faith means** trusting the yes's and the no's of God to work out His good, pleasing, and perfect will in His good, pleasing, and perfect time. God always sees further down the path. In fact, He knows the destination's end.

The Bible gives several references to the term "The just shall live by faith." This phrase is an admonition given unto all believers to live a life of faith in the **righteousness of Jesus Christ, our Savior**. "For therein is the righteousness of God revealed from faith to faith: as it is written, "The just shall live by faith" (Romans 1:17).

Therefore, when we **walk** by **faith** and not by **sight**, it is meaning that we are living life making decisions with a confident expectation that God will do what He has promised in His Word. We make decisions in life knowing that God is faithful, that we are loved, and that He has already given us the victory by faith.

This Victory, true victory today is mine because, Jesus gave it to me, way back on Calvary, when He died so that I could be free and have a right to the tree of life. It's something about knowing where victory and faith come from. Faith leads us to

- Live like Jesus Christ.
- Obey God's laws.
- Care for our families, Church members and others in need.
- Trust in God in good times and in fiery trials.
- Resist Satan.

These girls have witnessed faith and prayer in action that resulted in true victory. This is their conversation.

Tonya: Girls, I'm just so excited!

Stephanie: Why?

Crystal: What happened?

Tonya: Two of my friends just gave their lives to the Lord. I mean we had been praying for these two to come to the Lord.

Crystal: When, what and how? Tell me, tell me, tell me.

Tonya: Well, my one friend, the last time I saw her, and she was just walking the streets, living in cars, and going home with strange men. She looked bad. It looked like she had lost weight and she wasn't taking care of herself at all. But God, who is rich in mercy, save her, cleaned her up and took her off the streets and placed her in heavenly places with Christ Jesus. The other friend was on drugs and stealing. He couldn't keep a job. Growing up, he was very smart and handsome, but he couldn't take the pressure, I guess and turned to drugs. Now he's free from cocaine and he's born again. He's free from crack and he's ready for the devil's attack. God has got him, and He won't let go until he blesses him. I have to go because I invited them to go to Bible study with me tonight.

Crystal: Okay. That's great. I'll see you there.

Stephanie: God, if you save her friends, I know you can save mine. (*Hums the chorus of "I Am What I Am"* I am saved…. I am healed…. I'm forgiven and Holy Ghost Filled)

Something happens supernatural and divine when you witness the transforming power of God. A witness is **a person who has seen or can give first-hand evidence of some event.** To the modern world, a "**witness**" is commonly understood as someone who testifies on behalf of a person or to an event that he or she has seen with their own eyes or for which the person has first-hand knowledge. This is the common understanding of serving as a "**witness**" in court.

What does the Bible say about faithful witness?

Revelation 1:5 5 and from Jesus Christ, who is the faithful witness, the firstborn from the dead, and the ruler of the kings of the earth. To him who loves us and has freed us from our sins by his blood. The **true witness** of **Jesus Christ** are the Christians for they focus on the man and misses the His Spirit, but this **witness** is a false **witness**. The only **true witness** of **Christ** is the Spirit, and the Spirit is Truth and no apostle teacher prophet pastor can ever take that place.

What is a special witness of Christ?

To be a **special witness** of the name of **Christ** means that you have that **witness** and that authority that is unfailing, and it will be with you everywhere in the world.". Moses. He recounted a scriptural passage from the Pearl of Great Price. "Moses was carried away and saw all the Creation from beginning to end.

What is your testimony of Jesus Christ?

Chapter Eleven

Soul Praise In Service

Stephanie held on to her testimony of faith and now she can be a witness to the saving and transforming power of God through His Holy Spirit in the lives of those friends and family members that she prayed in faith for. Stephanie is on her way into the church when she meets her friend Billy on his way to pick up a Bible from Minister Alvin.

Stephanie: Billy, what are you doing here?

Billy: I tried to reach you at home, but I got no answer.

Stephanie: I'm surprised to see you here.

Billy: That's what I want to tell you. I was walking home earlier today and met Brother Alvin in the park and we started talking about the Lord and …I told him I wanted to be saved and now I am.

Stephanie: Oh Billy. You don't know how glad I am for you.

Billy: It sounds like they're ready to start (*he goes inside*)

Stephanie: (*talking to God*) Thank you Lord for reaching my friend (*she joins the praise service*

The Choir is singing a song: "I Will Rejoice" this is the day that the Lord has made. I will rejoice in it. Be glad for I have overcome. I will rejoice. One thing that I desired of the Lord that will I seek after. That I may dwell in the house of the Lord. To behold the beauty of the Lord. To inquire in His temple, the temple of the Lord. Oh, I want to see Him just to look upon His face. There to sing forever of His saving grace. Greater is He that is in me than he that is in the world. I can do all things through Christ because He is in control. I will enter His gates with thanksgiving. Thank You Jesus. I will enter His courts with praise. Hallelujah! I'll be thankful unto Him, I will bless His, bless His Holy Name! Bless His Holy Name!

Something happens when the people of God come together and rejoice. Praise is characterized as the act of magnifying and honoring God for who He is and the act of exalting God's great name. It also includes thanking God for his many kindnesses. Praise, in the original Greek, means **to sing, to tell of, to give, or to confess.** In simpler terms, it means to be thankful for God's blessings, and to declare that good news to God and to others. Praise is **a response of worship.** We sing boasts about the greatness of our God with purity and vigor. We proclaim His greatness to others in joy and excitement. True praise is **honest vocal adoration directed to God.** It means to adore or cherish Him. It also means to render Him divine honor and esteem, vocally! Praise is an action of expressed love to and for God. Praise is **an expression of approval or admiration.** We can praise people and we can praise God. In reference to God, praise is an acknowledgement and appreciation of what He has done for us.

The very first and primary reason for worship is to minister to the Lord. The basic posture of the worshiper is, "I will bless the Lord," not "Lord, bless me!" We all know this but let us face it—there are times when we go home from a worship service and complain because the worship did not do as much for us as it did last week. If the main purpose for worship is to bless and glorify the Lord, then why am I upset when it does not seem to bless me?

True praise comes from deep in the heart, and the outcome is that others see God working in us. Praise and worship are in fact to be the foundation on which we live our lives. Without both, we can't possibly be effective at being the hands and feet of God. To accomplish this, worship of God and of Him alone must be first priority at all times.

Truly Stephanie is used in Soul Thang as an Announcer to "Reach her Friends". This is The Gospel Played out in real time and in real life through God's Announcer.

an announcer
[ə'nounsər]
NOUN

What is an announcer? An announcer is a person who makes known something, in particular someone who introduces or gives information. A person who publishes and posts news and tidings.

An announcer – is someone who **proclaims a message publicly**. A communicator - a person who communicates with others. A caller - someone who proclaims or summons in a loud voice. Synonym Discussion of announce. declare, announce, **proclaim, promulgate mean to make known publicly**. declare implies explicitness and usually formality in making known.

We are called to the be announcers to our generation of the goodness and mercies of God. We are to announce His saving grace and to declare to this generation that Lord lives and blessed be the rock of our salvation. This is our soul thang. It is a real thing that has real results when reaching souls is our goal.

The human **soul** needs the protection, purification, and atonement of God. The human **soul** is eternal and imperishable, and every human **soul** will be somewhere for eternity.

Many people make goals. Three-to-five-year plans. Certainly, I have business and professional **goals**, but my **soul goals**, the things that will fulfill my heart and spirit, and make the world better, that's where I'm placing my focus. Goals for the soul can be spiritual or something that sustains your soul, which will give you a sense of peace and joy once you complete it, such as: delighting yourself in the Lord; trusting the Lord; studying the Word of God; having a vision of what life could/should be like living for the Lord; and **grow in the awareness** that the Lord does indeed fulfil His promise to be with us always. Another important goal is to win the lost at any cost.

God's power is upon those who are REDEEMED. Remember that Jesus told His disciples to go into all the world and to make disciples of all nations but also to teach them to observe what Jesus taught them. This is part of the seeking and saving of the lost. You will have to seek out the lost intentionally because they're not likely to come to you so you must go to them.

God could **have** chosen other methods to spread the gospel, and probably they would have been more effective. Angels could have done a better job, but God chose saved people to tell lost people the message. Be the ANNOUNCER to those who God sends your way. It's a "Soul Thang"!

What is your soul Goal?

Bibliography

Action Prayers, Poems and Songs for Children

A Heart A Flame—The Dynamic of Worship, Unknown Murchcison, Anne, Word Books, Waco, Texas, 1981

Almanac Dictionary

The Amplified Bible, grand Rapids, MI: Zondervan Publishing House, 1965

The Blue Bible Commentary Don Stewart

Bible Dictionary google.com

Boshman, Lamar The Rebirth of Music, Bedford, Texas, 1988

Capps, Charles, Angels, Harrison House, Tulsa, OK, 1984 Allen Ronald, Barclay,

Copyright © 2004 by Search Institute, 615 First Avenue NE, Suite 125, Minneapolis, MN 55413; 800-888-7828; www.search-institute.org.

Holman Old Testament Commentary

King James Version of the Bible

Law, Terry, The Power of Praise and Worship, Victory House Publishers, Tulsa, OK, 1984

The Living Bible

Matthew Henry Commentary

The Message Version of the Bible

New International Version of the Bible

New King James Version

Praise A Matter of Life and Breath, Thomas Nelson Publishers, 1975 Gills, James P. M.D.,

Samuel Butler (Stationer's Registry; Britain's Copyright, November 5, 1663.) "Hudibras"

Smith's Bible Dictionary, Thomas Nelson Publishers, 1962

Strong's Concordance

Victorious Life, Whetstone, Gary United States, Wilmington, Delaware, 1989

Webster's New collegiate dictionary, Springfield, MA: G&C Merriam Company, 1973

Soul Thang "Reach A Friend" The Characters

Stephanie (Sissy) Stevens

William "Billy" Nathaniel Brown III

Gossiper 1 Sister Melba Gasper

Gossiper 2 Sister Gabby Piper

Gossiper 3 Sister Alberta Riper

Gossiper 4 Sister Sangria Sipper

Deacon 1 Deacon Overly Downright

Deacon 2 Deacon Rodger Dodger

Brother Member Marvin Glover (D. L. Shack)

Sister Member Janice Dixon (Lady Shady)

Choir Members

Announcer Guest Charger

Church Clerk Gloria Gathers

Reverend Icha Nod Preacher

Church Usher Shirly Wally

Church Nurse Nancy Nailed

Neighbors Children at Playing

Vanessa Clark

Mrs. Suedette Stevens

Sheila Davis

Wanda Harris

Alvin Short "The Street Evangelist"

Tanya Jenkins

Crystal Strong

www.ingramcontent.com/pod-product-compliance
Lightning Source LLC
Chambersburg PA
CBHW031151250726

48655CB00002B/924